Date: 4/19/13

J 599.884 FRA
Franchino, Vicky.
Gorillas /

GORILLAS

by Vicky Franchino

Children's Press®

An Imprint of Scholastic Inc.

New York   Toronto   London   Auckland   Sydney
Mexico City   New Delhi   Hong Kong
Danbury, Connecticut

Content Consultant
Dr. Stephen S. Ditchkoff
Professor of Wildlife Sciences
Auburn University
Auburn, Alabama

Photographs © 2013: age fotostock: 8 (ARCO/C. Huetter), 5 top, 12
(Eric Baccega), 24 (FLPA/Paul Hobson), 19 (FLPA/Terry Whittaker), 36
(Photoshot); Alamy Images/Juniors Bildarchiv/F248: 7; Bob Italiano: 44
foreground, 45 foreground; Corbis Images/Bettmann: 35; Dreamstime:
1, 2, 46 (Eric Gevaert), 20 (Gilles Malo), 3, 44 background, 45
background (Radu Razvan Gheorghe); Getty Images: 27 (Gary Vestal),
4, 5 background, 40 (Konrad Wothe), cover (Steve Bloom), 28 (Victor
Estevez); Shutterstock, Inc.: 23 (Eric Gevaert), 16 (Fotomicar), 32
(Matej Hudovernik); Superstock, Inc.: 39 (age fotostock), 5 bottom, 11
(Gerard Lacz/age fotostock), 15, 31 (Minden Pictures).

Library of Congress Cataloging-in-Publication Data
Franchino, Vicky.
    Gorillas/by Vicky Franchino.
        p. cm.
    Includes bibliographical references and index.
    ISBN 978-0-531-20977-6 (library binding)
    ISBN 978-0-531-24303-9 (pbk.)
    1. Gorilla—Juvenile literature. I. Title.
    QL737.P96F72 2013
    599.884—dc23   2012030356

All rights reserved. Published in 2013
by Children's Press, an imprint of Scholastic Inc.

Printed in the United States of America 141
SCHOLASTIC, CHILDREN'S PRESS, and associated logos are
trademarks and/or registered trademarks of Scholastic Inc.

1 2 3 4 5 6 7 8 9 10 R 22 21 20 19 18 17 16 15 14 13

Gorillas

Class	Mammalia
Order	Primate
Family	Hominidae
Genus	*Gorilla*
Species	*Gorilla gorilla*
World distribution	Western and central Africa
Habitat	Tropical and mountain forests
Distinctive physical characteristics	Height of 5 to 6 feet (1.5 to 1.8 meters); weight can exceed 500 pounds (227 kilograms); has very long arms and walks on both feet and hands, using knuckles for balance; covered in dark fur; does not have a tail; has deep-set eyes, powerful jaws, and a cone-shaped head
Habits	Lives in a troop of 5 to 35 gorillas; nomadic lifestyle within a home range; extremely gentle except when threatened; uses noises and facial expressions to communicate
Diet	Largely herbivorous; eats vegetation of all kinds and occasionally grubs; gets its water from eating plants rather than drinking

Contents

6 CHAPTER 1
A Gentle Giant

13 CHAPTER 2
Life in the Jungle

18 CHAPTER 3
One Big, Happy Family

29 CHAPTER 4
Apes Past and Present

34 CHAPTER 5
An Endangered Species

42 Words to Know

44 Habitat Map

46 Find Out More

47 Index

48 About the Author

A Gentle Giant

As the sun rises over the horizon, another day begins in the jungles of Africa. Out of the grass, a dark shadow rises. Huge and covered in fur, the creature is a fearsome sight. As it makes its way through the tall grass, it is soon obvious that this is not one creature, but two. It is a mother gorilla and her child. The infant nestles into the front of its mother. The adult gorilla cuddles her close. What seemed like a terrifying monster is really just a loving mother and her baby.

For many years, explorers traveled home from Africa with stories of the jungle's most frightening creature. And for a long time, people believed that gorillas were violent and terrifying. It is only in the last century that scientists have studied gorillas enough to see that just the opposite is true. Today we know that gorillas are actually extremely gentle.

Baby gorillas rarely stray far from their mothers.

Not as Scary as They Seem

One reason that people find gorillas so frightening is their size. Male gorillas can weigh up to 500 pounds (227 kilograms) and be up to 6 feet (1.8 meters) tall. Females can weigh as much as 200 pounds (91 kg) and grow to heights of 5 feet (1.5 m). Gorillas are the largest members of the primate family. This group includes monkeys, apes, and other similar animals.

A gorilla has a large head, and a huge belly. Most of a gorilla's large body is covered with thick hair. Only its face, chest, palms of the hands, and bottoms of the feet are hairless.

A gorilla will make terrifying noises and throw things if it feels that danger is nearby. Although this could all seem very scary to someone who crosses paths with a gorilla, the truth is that gorillas like to bluff. They may pretend to be fierce to protect themselves and their families, but most gorillas would rather avoid trouble than start it.

Adult Male
6 ft. (1.8 m)

Male Gorilla
6 ft. (1.8 m)

Gorillas can look very frightening when they are angry.

Western and Eastern Gorillas

There is only one species of gorilla. However, there are three different subspecies. The western lowland gorilla and the eastern lowland gorilla both live in the rain forests of the Congo Basin in Africa. The western lowland gorilla ranges from the Congo River northwest into the country of Cameroon. It is the type of gorilla most often seen in zoos. Eastern lowland gorillas live in the rain forest of the Democratic Republic of the Congo.

The easiest way to tell these two subspecies apart is to look at their upper bodies. Western lowland gorillas have narrower chests and shorter faces than their eastern cousins. They also have lighter brown hair on their heads.

The third subspecies is called the mountain gorilla. It lives high up in the forest-covered mountains of central Africa. Mountain gorillas have long, heavy fur. This helps them stay warm in their chilly, high-altitude home.

Lowland gorillas, such as this one, have shorter fur than mountain gorillas.

CHAPTER 2

Life in the Jungle

A gorilla spends much of its day hunting for food. It has 32 teeth and strong jaws. These allow the gorilla to chew up the roots and plants that make up most of its diet. Gorillas have a high bony ridge at the back of their head that supports the muscles of these powerful jaws. It is called a sagittal crest.

A gorilla's diet is usually made up of fruits, vegetables, and plants. Gorillas sometimes eat insects and grubs, too. It takes a lot of plants to fill up a hungry gorilla. Gorillas often eat more than 40 pounds (18 kg) of food a day. They have long, thick **intestines** to help process all that food. A gorilla's belly is much wider than its chest because it must hold these long intestines.

Gorillas can be fussy eaters. They use their fingers to pick out their favorite parts of a plant. Gorillas don't need to worry about finding water to drink. They get most of the water they need from the plants they eat.

Gorillas eat huge amounts of leaves and other plant parts.

Designed for Survival

Gorillas have eyes that point forward. This means they can use both eyes to look at one thing. Because of this, a gorilla can easily tell how far away something is. A bony ridge juts out from a gorilla's forehead and protects its eyes.

Gorillas have a good sense of smell. They use it to tell the difference between a stranger and a familiar gorilla. Male gorillas have special glands under their arms that can produce a strong odor. This scent helps to signal others when danger is near.

Hearing is very important to gorillas. In a dark forest where the trees and leaves block out the sun, it can be hard for a gorilla to see where the other members of its group have gone. A gorilla will listen carefully for the sound of familiar friends. Some primatologists believe that a young gorilla can recognize the sound of its mother's voice.

A gorilla's eyes are protected by the ridge on its forehead.

Moving On

A gorilla might stand up on two legs if it wants to scare off an intruder. But it usually walks on both its legs and its hands. Instead of using the bottom of its palms, a gorilla will lean forward and walk on its knuckles.

A gorilla's arms are longer and stronger than its legs. The gorilla uses these powerful arms to support its large upper body. It also uses these strong arms to lift or break heavy objects that get in its way.

Gorillas don't travel very quickly. They also don't travel very far. During a single day they will usually move less than 0.5 miles (0.8 km) from where they started. They might need to travel farther if they can't find enough food.

Gorillas spend most of their time on the ground. However, they sometimes climb trees to play, sleep, or search for a special treat such as a juicy piece of fruit.

FUN FACT! When knuckle-walking, gorillas support their weight on two fingers of each hand.

Gorillas use their long arms to travel across a variety of terrain.

CHAPTER 3

One Big, Happy Family

Gorillas are very social animals. They live in **troops** of between 5 and 35 gorillas. The troop is led by an older male gorilla called a silverback. It also includes younger males known as blackbacks, females, and their offspring.

The silverback makes all the decisions for the troop. He decides where the troop will look for food and when it will stop to sleep for the night. The silverback also protects the troop and is usually the father of all the troop's babies.

Each day, the troop moves around its **home range** looking for food and a place to spend the night. A home range usually covers between 1 and 16 square miles (2.6 to 41 square kilometers).

When it is time to stop for the night, gorillas make nests out of grass. Younger gorillas might climb into the trees to sleep, but older gorillas usually stay on the ground. A troop never sleeps in the same place twice. Some experts believe that this is because the gorillas want to sleep in clean nests every night.

Traveling in groups makes it easier for gorillas to find food and protect their young.

A Troop of Their Own

When a female gorilla becomes an adult, she sometimes moves from one troop to another until she finds one she likes. She tries to find a troop with a strong silverback who will protect her and her children.

Although some animals stay with the same partner for life, this is not true for gorillas. The silverback **mates** with many of the females in his troop.

Adult females usually have one baby every three or four years, starting when they are about 10 years old. Males usually begin reproducing when they are between 15 and 20 years old, though some start when they are younger.

When a female gorilla is ready to mate, her body produces a special odor that attracts a male. Once she has a baby, she usually stays with this troop for the rest of her life.

Mother gorillas share very close relationships with their children.

Bringing Up Baby

Baby gorillas and baby humans have a lot in common. They both grow inside their mother's body for about nine months, and they are both helpless at birth. A newborn gorilla weighs about 4 pounds (2 kg). A human baby weighs about twice that much.

Gorillas are very good parents. Both the mother and the father care for and play with the baby. The mother **nurses** the gorilla baby until it is about two years old. A young gorilla often sleeps in its mother's nest until it is four to six years old.

When mother and baby need to travel, the baby climbs on the mother's back and holds on tight. Gorillas learn how to walk when they are about six months old, but they might still get a piggyback ride when they need to travel quickly or there is danger.

FUN FACT! Every gorilla has a unique nose shape. No two are exactly alike!

Baby gorillas often hitch a ride on their mother's back.

Life in the Troop

Young gorillas spend much of their time climbing and wrestling. This might look like play, but it also teaches them the skills they will need as adults.

Gorillas learn how to survive in the wild by watching older troop members. They discover what to eat by following their mother and watching her. If she picks and eats something, the young gorillas know that it is safe for them too.

When they are between the ages of three and six, gorillas are called juveniles. They are considered adults when they are about eight years old.

Once gorillas are adults, they start their own troops or join an existing troop. Sometimes a male will attract females from another troop. Other times, a younger male will try to take over a troop from an older silverback. There have been troops with more than one silverback, but this is very rare.

Young gorillas climb trees much more often than adults do.

Something to Talk About

Gorillas are excellent communicators. Although they don't use actual words, they do use their voices. Scientists who have worked closely with gorillas believe they can make more than 20 different noises. When a gorilla wants to scare off an intruder, it stands up tall to make itself look scary. It then gives a big hoot and makes a loud thumping sound by beating its chest with cupped hands. These noises can carry over a long distance.

Gorillas also use facial expressions to communicate. Many look just like the ones that humans use. A gorilla might smile when it is happy or frown when it is upset. But don't be fooled by a yawn. A yawn doesn't mean that a gorilla is tired. It means that it is worried or nervous!

FUN FACT! Wild gorillas usually live for around 35 years. Captive gorillas can live even longer.

Gorillas can make many different sounds and facial expressions.

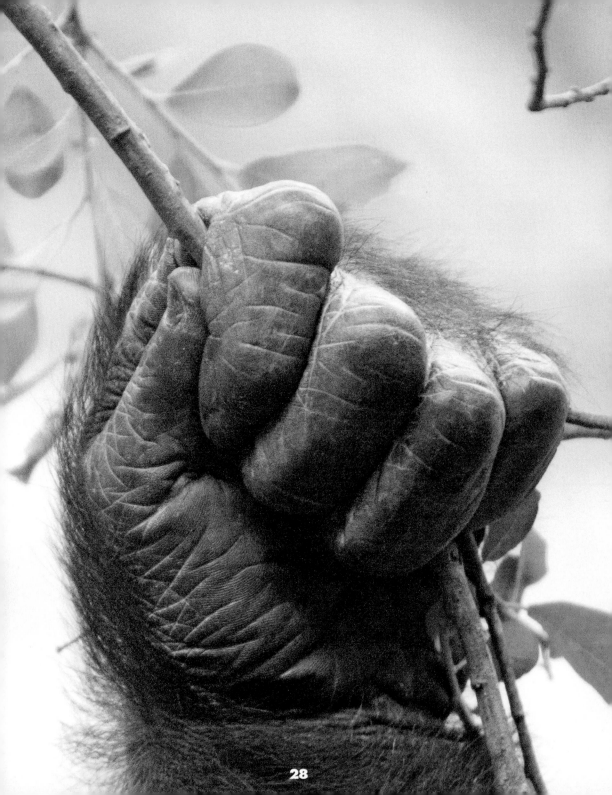

CHAPTER 4

Apes Past and Present

If you compare the skeleton of a human with the skeleton of a gorilla, you will notice many similarities. Scientists believe that humans and gorillas had a common ancestor. About 7 million to 8 million years ago, the branch of animals that became gorillas split off from the branch that became humans.

DNA research has shown just how similar gorillas and humans are. DNA is a material in an animal's cells that acts like a code. This code controls traits such as height and eye color. Because humans and gorillas share about 98 percent of their DNA, they have many things in common.

For instance, gorillas have four fingers and an opposable thumb on each hand. This thumb allows them to pick up and hold on to objects just as humans do. Gorillas' fingers have nails and one-of-a-kind fingerprints, just like humans have. Gorillas are very smart. They can solve problems and learn new things. They can even figure out how to use sticks and rocks as tools.

Gorillas have thumbs that allow them to grasp objects just as humans do.

Chimps and Bonobos

Many people believe gorillas are related to monkeys, but they are actually different types of primates. One big difference is that gorillas do not have tails, while monkeys do. Gorillas belong to the same family as chimpanzees, bonobos, orangutans, and gibbons.

Chimps have a lot in common with gorillas. They communicate with noises and facial expressions, and have figured out how to use tools. They are very smart. Scientists have been able to teach chimpanzees how to use sign language and computers. Chimpanzees are also different from gorillas. Unlike gorillas, they sometimes eat meat and live in larger groups.

Scientists once believed bonobos to be a subspecies of chimpanzees. However, bonobos and chimpanzees are now considered to be two separate species.

Bonobos, which are extremely endangered, are also very similar to gorillas. Like gorillas, bonobos eat plants and fruit. Unlike gorillas, they also eat fish and other small animals. Their troops are led by females.

Bonobos look a lot like chimpanzees, but they are a separate species.

Orangutans and Gibbons

Orangutans and gibbons are two ape species that live in Asia. Like gorillas, the male orangutan is larger than the female. A male weighs up to 200 pounds (91 kg) and can reach heights of 4.5 feet (1.4 m). Females are about half that size. Orangutan mothers and their babies live together, while males usually live alone. Males have large pouches by their throats. They use these pouches to make loud sounds. An orangutan's arms are longer than its height. These long limbs let them climb and swing in trees. On the ground, orangutans have a special way of walking on the edges of their feet.

Gibbons live in small family groups with a father, mother, and children. They are the smallest of the apes. They weigh just 15 pounds (7 kg) and are usually less than 3 feet (0.9 m) tall. Gibbons can communicate by song. There are different songs for male and female gibbons. Sometimes they sing a duet. Scientists believe that gibbons use these songs to mark their territory.

Orangutans' red fur helps them stand out from other great ape species.

CHAPTER 5

An Endangered Species

To learn more about gorillas and help protect them from threats, scientists have conducted many studies of this endangered species. During the late 1950s and early 1960s, George Schaller became the first scientist to live in Africa and study gorillas. His research showed that gorillas are gentle and clever.

Another researcher, Dian Fossey, lived in Africa among the gorillas from 1966 to 1985. She found that the gorillas would accept her if she acted like them. She began to copy their actions. She thumped her chest, pretended to eat the same food, and made the same noises. It worked! The gorillas accepted Fossey and she learned many new things.

In captivity, some gorillas have learned how to communicate with humans. A famous gorilla named Koko learned American Sign Language. Koko can sign more than 1,000 words and understand about 2,000 spoken English words.

Dr. Penny Patterson taught Koko to communicate using sign language.

The Human Threat

Even though scientists have devoted a great deal of time to studying and protecting gorillas, these apes still face many dangers. Gorillas have very few natural enemies in the wild. The biggest threats to their survival come from humans.

Humans clear the gorillas' forest homes to grow crops and build roads and houses. Scientists estimate that millions of acres of African forests disappear every year. This loss of habitat means gorillas can't find food or a safe place to live.

In some areas, gorillas die because they are exposed to human diseases. Sometimes tourists come into the gorillas' forests. Other times, people move into areas where gorillas live. They can bring diseases that the gorillas don't have any protection against.

Gorillas are also threatened by war and conflict. Many of the African countries where gorillas live have seen heavy fighting in recent decades. Sometimes people escape to the gorillas' forests for safety. Other times, there is actual fighting in the areas set aside for the gorillas. Park rangers cannot defend the gorillas in these dangerous conditions.

Logging is a major danger to gorilla habitats.

The Problem with Poaching

Poachers also threaten gorillas. Some kill gorillas for meat. Bushmeat, which is the meat from wild animals, is popular in restaurants and with the people who live in the forest.

Others kill gorillas for sport. This is illegal in many African countries, but that doesn't always stop the poachers. A dead gorilla makes a valuable trophy for them. Sometimes gorillas are killed by accident when they are caught in traps set for other animals.

There are people who believe that a gorilla's body parts will give them special powers. They are willing to pay a lot of money for these body parts. Other people think gorillas make interesting pets and don't care that it is illegal to capture them.

FUN FACT! Gorilla hands, feet, and skulls are all sold illegally as lucky charms.

Some people hunt gorillas because they see these sometimes fierce-looking animals as challenging targets.

A Future for Gorillas

Many groups want to help gorillas, but it can be dangerous and difficult work. Poachers make a lot of money from illegally capturing or killing gorillas. They might hurt or kill people who try to stop them. The areas where gorillas live are often quite large and hard to get to.

Some African governments have passed laws to protect the gorillas. Others have set up reserves where gorillas can live in peace. These reserves can help to protect the gorillas and their habitat. They can also provide jobs for people who live in the area. This might give people fewer reasons to illegally hunt gorillas. Unfortunately, these laws and safe areas aren't always respected, especially in times of war and fighting. Even though it will be a long and difficult struggle, it is up to humans to protect these special creatures from disappearing forever.

Parks and reserves provide safe places for gorillas to live.

Words to Know

altitude (AL-ti-tood) — height above ground or sea level

ancestor (AN-ses-tur) — an ancient animal species that is related to a modern species

captivity (kap-TIV-i-tee) — the condition of being held or trapped by people

century (SEN-chur-ee) — a period of 100 years

DNA (DEE EN AY) — the molecule that carries genes, found inside the nucleus of cells

endangered (en-DAYN-jurd) — at risk of becoming extinct, usually because of human activity

family (FAM-uh-lee) — a group of living things that are related to each other

glands (GLANDZ) — organs in the body that produce natural chemicals

habitat (HAB-uh-tat) — the place where an animal or a plant is usually found

home range (HOME RAYNJ) — area of land in which animals spend most of their time

intestines (in-TES-tinz) — long tubes in the body extending below the stomach that digest food

mates (MAYTZ) — joins together to produce babies

nurses (NURS-ez) — feeds a baby milk from a breast

opposable thumb (uh-POHZ-uh-buhl THUM) — a digit that is able to move against the other digits on a hand or foot

poachers (POH-churz) — people who hunt or fish illegally

primatologists (pry-muh-TAH-luh-jists) — scientists who study primates

reserves (ri-ZURVZ) — protected places where hunting is not allowed and where animals can live and breed safely

species (SPEE-sheez) — one of the groups into which animals and plants of the same genus are divided

subspecies (SUHB-spee-sheez) — groups of animals that are part of the same species, but share important differences

territory (TER-i-tor-ee) — area of land claimed by an animal

troops (TROOPS) — groups of gorillas that live and travel together

Habitat Map

NORTH AMERICA

PACIFIC

OCEAN

ATLANTIC

SOUTH AMERICA

Gorilla Range

ARCTIC OCEAN

EUROPE

ASIA

AFRICA

PACIFIC OCEAN

INDIAN OCEAN

OCEAN

AUSTRALIA

CAMEROON

GABON

CONGO

DEMOCRATIC REPUBLIC OF THE CONGO

45

Find Out More

Books

Gish, Melissa. *Gorillas.* Mankato, MN: Creative Education, 2011.

Goldish, Meish. *Gorillas.* New York: Bearport Publishing, 2007.

Turner, Pamela S. *Gorilla Doctors: Saving Endangered Great Apes.* Boston: Houghton Mifflin, 2005.

Visit this Scholastic Web site for more information on gorillas:
www.factsfornow.scholastic.com
Enter the keyword **Gorillas**

Index

Page numbers in *italics* indicate a photograph or map.

adulthood, 21, 25
aggression, 6, *8*, 9, 17, 26, *39*
ancestors, 29
arms, 14, *16*, 17, 33

babies, 6, *7*, 14, 18, *20*, 21, 22, *23*
blackbacks, 18
bonobos, 30, *31*
bushmeat, 38

captivity, 10, 26, 34, 38
chimpanzees, 30
climbing, 17, 18, *24*, 25, 33
colors, 10, 29, *32*
communication, 9, 14, 21, 26, *27*, 30, 33, 34, *35*

digestion, 13
diseases, 37
DNA research, 29

eastern lowland gorillas, 10
endangered species, 30, 34
eyes, 14, *15*, 29

facial expressions, 26, *27*, 30
females, 6, *7*, 9, 14, 18, *20*, 21, 22, *23*, 25, 30, 33
fingers, 13, 29
food, *12*, 13, 17, 18, 22, 25, 30, 34, 37
forehead ridges, 14, *15*

Fossey, Dian, 34
fur, 6, 9, 10, *11*, *32*

gibbons, 30, 33

habitats, 6, 10, *36*, 37, *40*, 41
hearing, 14
home ranges, 18
hunting, 38, *39*, 41

intelligence, 29, 30
intestines, 13

jaws, 13
juveniles, 25

Koko, 34, *35*

laws, 41
legs, 17
life span, 26
logging, *36*, 37
lowland gorillas, 10, *11*

males, 9, *9*, 14, 18, 21, 22, 25, 33
mating, 18, 21
mountain gorillas, 10

nests, 18, 22
noises. *See* communication.
noses, 22

(Index continued)

nursing, 22

orangutans, 30, *32*, 33

people, 6, 9, 26, 29, 33, 34, *35*, 37, 38, 41
pets, 38
playing, 17, 22, 25
poachers, 38, 41
primate family, 9, 30

reserves, *40*, 41

scents, 14, 21
senses, 14
sign language, 30, 34, *35*
silverbacks, 18, 21, 25
sizes, 9, *9*, 26, 33
skeletons, 29

sleeping, 17, 18, 22
species, 10, 30, 33
subspecies, 10, 30

teeth, 13
territory, 33
thumbs, *28*, 29
tools, 29, 30
travel, *16*, 17, *19*, 22, *23*
troops, 18, *19*, 21, 25, 30

war, 37, 41
water, 13
weight, 9, 22, 33
western lowland gorillas, 10
wrestling, 25

zoos, 10

About the Author

Vicky Franchino has written dozens of books for children and always enjoys getting to learn interesting new facts about the world around her. She had no idea that gorillas are so gentle and was especially interested to find out how they can communicate with people. Did you know that Koko the gorilla called her cat "All Ball" because she didn't have a tail? (You can look it up in the book *Koko's Kitten*!.) Vicky lives in Madison, Wisconsin, with her husband and daughters.